The Death Penalty

Identifying Propaganda Techniques

The Death Penalty

Identifying Propaganda Techniques

Curriculum Consultant: JoAnne Buggey, Ph.D.
College of Education, University of Minnesota

By Carol O'Sullivan

Greenhaven Press, Inc.
Post Office Box 289009
San Diego, CA 92128-9009

Titles in the opposing viewpoints juniors series:

Smoking	Death Penalty
Gun Control	Drugs and Sports
Animal Rights	Toxic Wastes
AIDS	Patriotism
Alcohol	Working Mothers
Immigration	Terrorism

Cover photo: Wide World Photos

Library of Congress Cataloging-in-Publication Data

O'Sullivan, Carol, 1945–
    The death penalty : identifying propaganda techniques / by Carol O'Sullivan.
        p.   cm. — (Opposing viewpoints juniors)
    ISBN 0-89908-494-X :
    1. Capital punishment—Juvenile literature.   [2. Critical thinking—Juvenile literature.   3. Propaganda—Juvenile literature.
    I. Title.   II. Series.
    HV8694.07 1989
    364.6′6—dc20   89-11033
                                                                    CIP
                                                                    AC

CONTENTS

An Introduction to
Opposing Viewpoints

When people disagree, it is hard to figure out who is right. You may decide one person is right just because the person is your friend or relative. But this is not a very good reason to agree or disagree with someone. It is better if you try to understand why these people disagree. On what main points do they differ? Read or listen to each person's argument carefully. Separate the facts and opinions that each person presents. Finally, decide which argument best matches what you think. This process, examining an argument without emotion, is part of what critical thinking is all about.

This is not easy. Many things make it hard to understand and form opinions. People's values, ages, and experiences all influence the way they think. This is why learning to read and think critically is an invaluable skill. Opposing Viewpoints Juniors books will help

you learn and practice skills to improve your ability to read critically. By reading opposing views on an issue, you will become familiar with methods people use to attempt to convince you that their point of view is right. And you will learn to separate the authors' opinions from the facts they present.

Each Opposing Viewpoints Juniors book focuses on one critical thinking skill that will help you judge the views presented. Some of these skills are telling fact from opinion, recognizing propaganda techniques, and locating and analyzing the main idea. These skills will allow you to examine opposing viewpoints more easily.

Each viewpoint in this book is paraphrased from the original to make it easier to read. The viewpoints are placed in a running debate and are always placed with the pro view first.

What Are Propaganda Techniques?

Propaganda is information presented in an attempt to influence people. In this Opposing Viewpoints Juniors book, you will be asked to identify and study several common propaganda techniques. Some of these techniques appeal to your ability to think logically, while others appeal to your emotions. As an example, a car saleswoman who is telling you about a small economy car may say, "This car gets much better gas mileage than any car in its class." The saleswoman's argument for buying the car is based on her belief that you will make your car-buying decision logically. You will compare practical considerations such as mileage and initial cost. Another example is a car salesman who is telling you about a snazzy Maserati: "This car is the best-looking, fastest car ever made." His argument for buying the Maserati is based on his belief that you are considering such a car not for its practical qualities but because it excites you and is a status symbol.

In the examples above, the objective of both salespeople is to encourage you to buy a car. Both try to get you to focus on the most appealing quality of their cars—economy in the first example, flashiness in the second. Both ignore the disadvantages of their cars. In both cases, making a wise buying decision would mean getting more information. Since the car salespeople's objective is to get you to buy *their* car, you would need more objective sources, such as *Consumer Reports* magazine, to find out more facts.

DISTRACTING THE READER

All propaganda techniques, like those used by the car salespeople, distract the listener or reader from the complete picture. People who use propaganda techniques encourage you to look only at the factors that are important to accepting their argument as true.

Authors and speakers often use misleading propaganda techniques instead of offering legitimate proof for their arguments. The propaganda will be offered as a reason to believe the argument, but in reality will be weak, distracting, or irrelevant reasons. This Opposing Viewpoints Juniors book will focus on telling the difference between legitimate reasons to believe a particular argument and propaganda techniques that are used to mislead or distract you.

It is important to learn to recognize these techniques, especially when reading and evaluating differing opinions. This is because people who feel strongly about an issue use many of these techniques when attempting to persuade others to agree with their opinion. Some of these persuasive techniques may be relevant to your decision to agree, but others will not be. It is important to sift through the information, weeding the proof from the false reasoning.

While there are many types of propaganda techniques, this book will focus on three of them. These are *testimonial, bandwagon,* and *scare tactics.* Examples of these techniques are given below:

Testimonial—quoting or paraphrasing a celebrity or person in authority to support one's own argument. Often, the person being quoted is not qualified to express an opinion on the subject. For example, movie stars are often used to recommend a product they may know nothing about.

Sometimes, an actor or actress is dressed to look like an authority on the subject. For example, an actor will be dressed in a doctor's coat to recommend a pain medication in a TV commercial. The producers of the commercial believe you will assume the actor in a white coat is a doctor. They hope you will buy the pain medication because you trust doctors' opinions. But the truth is that the actor is not a doctor, has no knowledge of medicine, and is in no position to express an opinion. The commercial is deceptive—it asks you to accept the advice of someone who is not in a position to express an informed opinion.

But not all testimonials are used deceptively. Quoting a person who is truly an authority is a good way to support an argument. For instance, quoting a famous comedian like Richard Pryor about how drugs almost ruined his life would be an example of using a testimonial properly. He is in a position to give advice based on his personal experience. Also, quoting a dentist about how to prevent tooth decay is an example of a legitimate, or genuine, testimonial.

Bandwagon—suggesting that everybody else, or most people, or everybody in a certain group believes or acts a certain way, and therefore you should too. Bandwagon is a form of peer pressure that plays on a person's desire to be liked and respected. An example is, "Most people in our neighborhood have signed this petition to have a movie theater built. You should sign it, too."

Bandwagon arguments appeal to your sense of being part of the group, of being accepted. The purpose is to persuade you to do something just because everyone else is doing it. In the above example, the speaker tries to get you to sign a petition just because everyone else has signed it. But this is never a good reason to do something or believe something. You should consider all the evidence in a logical way and then decide for yourself. Whatever you decide, it should be your own opinion. It should not be based solely on what everyone else thinks is right.

Scare tactic—the threat that if you do not do or believe this, something terrible will happen. People using this technique will write or say alarming words and phrases to persuade you to believe their arguments. For example:

> Outer space has become our newest dumping ground.
> If we do not stop leaving pieces of rockets and other
> space junk in outer space, the sun will not be able to
> shine through our atmosphere. Without sunlight, we
> would die.

This is a deceptive argument. Considering the vastness of outer space and the power of the sun, it is unlikely that space debris could keep the sun from shining onto the earth. And no evidence is offered that this would be the case.

Authors who use scare tactics will often make up or exaggerate the frightening aspects of an issue. They want you to make a decision about the issue based on fear rather than on sound reasoning.

When reading differing arguments, then, there is a lot to think about. Are the authors giving sound reasons for their points of view? Or do they distort the importance of their arguments with propaganda techniques?

We asked two students to give their opinions on the death penalty issue. Look for examples of testimonial, bandwagon, and scare tactics in their arguments.

I think the death penalty is good.

I think the death penalty is the best punishment for murderers. My grandmother told me the Bible says "an eye for an eye, a tooth for a tooth." She says this means God thinks it's right to kill a person who has killed someone else.

I think the death penalty keeps people from killing other people. People would be afraid to kill someone because they would not want to be put to death.

There's another reason to kill murderers. By killing them, we make sure that they cannot murder anyone else. Sometimes murderers don't spend very much time in jail. Sometimes they even get to go home on weekends. The streets are probably full of murderers. Maybe they're looking for someone else to kill.

I think the death penalty is bad.

It's impossible to be sure someone is guilty of committing a crime. My friend Brian has an uncle who was blamed for killing someone. He almost had to go to the electric chair. Luckily, someone else confessed to the murder before Brian's uncle died. But if that person hadn't confessed, Brian's uncle would be dead today.

My dad says there's another reason for not letting the government kill people. He says the government already has too much power. Dad says soon the government will start telling us where we can live, what jobs we can do, and what books we can read.

Most other countries have stopped using the death penalty. These countries have lots of smart people who have thought about what's right and what's wrong. I think the United States should follow these countries and stop killing people.

Chip and Naomi have very different opinions about the death penalty. Both of them use propaganda techniques in their arguments:

Chip:

TESTIMONIAL

My grandmother told me the Bible says "an eye for an eye, a tooth for a tooth." She says this means God thinks it's right to kill a person who has killed someone else.

SCARE TACTIC

The streets are probably full of murderers.

Naomi:

TESTIMONIAL

My dad says there is another reason for not letting the government kill people. He says the government already has too much power.

BANDWAGON

Most other countries have stopped using the death penalty. . . . I think the United States should follow these countries and stop killing people.

In this sample, Chip and Naomi use some propaganda techniques when presenting their opinions. Both Chip and Naomi think they are right about the death penalty. What would you conclude about the death penalty from this sample? Why? As you continue to read through the viewpoints in this book, try keeping a tally like the one above to compare the authors' arguments.

CHAPTER 1

PREFACE: Should the Death Penalty Be Abolished?

A hotly-debated issue in our society is whether a person who commits a brutal crime, such as murder, should be punished by death.

The death penalty, also called "capital punishment," is not new to the United States. During most of the seventeenth and eighteenth centuries, the American colonies were under British rule. At that time, 200 different crimes were punishable by death. Among these crimes were stealing a loaf of bread and insulting the Crown.

The laws have softened since the eighteenth century. Criminals are no longer executed for petty crimes. But many people argue that executing criminals for any crime is wrong. These people claim that the death penalty should be abolished, or ended, because it is not only immoral but also illegal. They say it violates the Eighth Amendment to the Constitution. This amendment forbids cruel and unusual punishments. It is stated as follows:

> Excessive bail shall not be required, nor excessive fines imposed, nor cruel and unusual punishments inflicted.

On the other side are people who favor the death penalty. These people claim that executing criminals is neither cruel nor unusual as long as the criminals do not suffer physical pain. Those who favor the death penalty further argue that it does no good to put murderers in jail. Society is not protected from them because they get released from jail in a few years. Then they are back on the streets committing more crimes.

The death penalty is an emotional issue. Arguments for and against it use many propaganda techniques. In the next two viewpoints, look for examples of testimonial, scare tactics, and bandwagon.

The death penalty should be abolished

Editor's Note: This viewpoint is paraphrased from an article written by a member of Amnesty International. Amnesty International is a human rights organization that opposes the death penalty. In this viewpoint, the author tells why the death penalty should be ended.

More and more prisoners in the United States are being executed for their crimes. At least sixty-six people have been executed since 1976. Nearly two thousand more are on death row. They are waiting to be electrocuted, gassed, poisoned, hanged, or shot.

It is true that most of the criminals on death row have been convicted of brutal crimes. But killing a person is not proper punishment for any crime. It is a violation of the basic right to life. And, it is illegal. The Constitution of the United States forbids cruel and unusual punishment. Robbing a person of his or her life is certainly cruel and unusual.

Besides ending their lives, executions also cause prisoners physical pain. This, too, is cruel and unusual. Some examples of this suffering are:

> In a 1983 electrocution in Alabama, three charges of nineteen hundred volts of electricity and fourteen minutes were needed to kill the prisoner. After the second charge, smoke and flames burst from his head and left leg.

> In a 1983 execution by poisonous gas in Mississippi, the prisoner shook violently for eight minutes. He kept hitting his head on a pole behind him before he died.

"Fetch me the law for the rich, will you?"

© Punch/Rothco

This cruelty is reason enough to put an end to the death penalty. But there is another reason. The death penalty is not handed out fairly. The evidence suggests that the use of the death penalty has become a horrifying "lottery." Luck and the circumstances of a person's life often determine whether he or she will live or die.

For example, it is not fair that poor people are executed a lot more often than rich people. In fact, a former governor of Ohio said, "I have found that men on death row had one thing in common: they were penniless . . . the fact that they had no money was a principal factor in their being condemned to death." This belief is also expressed by a former warden of San Quentin prison in California. He said that the death penalty is "a privilege of the poor."

Also, it is not fair that people with mental illness are often not even aware that they have done anything wrong. Yet, many are executed right along with people who know right from wrong.

Finally, it is not fair that when two people commit a crime, sometimes only one person is executed for it. In one case, a prisoner was executed for murder even though his partner committed the crime. The prisoner was not even in the room when the killing happened. But the court said the prisoner was guilty because he should have known his partner was capable of killing. In another case, a killer's partner was executed for a murder while the killer himself was given only a life sentence.

Perhaps the most important reason for ending the death penalty is that innocent people are sometimes executed. Records show that at least twenty-three people in the United States have been killed for crimes they did not commit.

Executions in the United States are increasing. However, in the rest of the civilized world, they are decreasing. Many other countries are completely doing away with the death penalty. France ended the death penalty in 1981. Britain ended it in 1969. In fact, at least one country a year has put an end to the death penalty since 1975. It is time the United States did the same.

The author says the death penalty is handed out unfairly. Does he offer proof that this is the case? Is this a scare tactic?

Does the governor's testimonial persuade you to agree with the author that the death penalty should be abolished? Why or why not?

Do you think a prison warden knows which prisoners are most often executed? Is he in a position to give an informed opinion on the death penalty? Why or why not?

The author tells us that many other countries are getting rid of the death penalty and that the United States should too. Which propaganda technique is he using?

Is the death penalty handed out unfairly?

The author gives four reasons for why the death penalty is handed out unfairly. Can you name these four reasons? Which of these four reasons is the most convincing? Why?

The death penalty should not be abolished

Editor's Note: This viewpoint is paraphrased from an article that appeared in *Lincoln Review* journal. In it, the author explains why the death penalty is needed in America and why arguments against the death penalty are weak.

The death penalty is being debated in the United States. Because many people oppose the death penalty, few murderers have been executed. The result is that murder has become an epidemic in our society.

The author says murder has become an epidemic in our society. Is he using a scare tactic? Why or why not?

More people are murdered in the U.S. than have been killed in some war zones. For example, during the German bombardment of London in the years 1940–1945, there were 21.7 deaths per 100,000 people. In Detroit, for the years 1973–1978, there were 42.4 deaths per 100,000 people from murder.

People who oppose the death penalty cite many reasons for wanting to end this form of punishment. They argue that the death penalty violates the Eighth Amendment to the Constitution. This amendment forbids using cruel or unusual methods to punish criminals.

But people who use the Eighth Amendment argument forget an important fact. This amendment was made part of the Constitution in 1791. At that time, governments throughout the world did punish criminals cruelly and unusually.

One of these methods of punishment was burning the victim. Another method was impaling—throwing the victim on a sharp stake. A third method was pressing—piling rocks on top of the victim until he or she could not breathe. But today, Americans do not use cruel forms of punishment. Therefore, modern executions in the United States do not violate the Eighth Amendment.

Opponents of the death penalty have another reason for wanting to end it. They say killing a human being for any reason is immoral. These people argue that executing murderers is against the religious tradition of America.

But C. S. Lewis, a Christian writer, disagrees. He says that the "human feeling that bad men ought to suffer" does not go against our religious beliefs. And St. Paul wrote that governments are appointed by God to carry out His punishment. Therefore, the government is doing God's will by executing murderers. Finally, Jesus Christ said, "All who take the sword will perish by the sword." This can be interpreted to mean Jesus thought that murderers deserve to die.

People who think the death penalty is immoral say that putting a murderer in prison for life is punishment enough. But there is a problem with this punishment. Most murderers sentenced to life in prison are released. In New York, prisoners serving life sentences can be released in just nineteen months.

Robert Johnson, assistant professor of justice at American University's School of Justice, said that most criminals are no longer given true life sentences. He said that most prisoners convicted of murder serve only seven to fourteen years in jail.

People who oppose the death penalty have one more reason for wanting to end it. They say that fear of the death penalty does not stop murderers from killing their victims. This may be true in some cases. But most people, including murderers, are afraid to die. Ernest van den Haag, a professor at Fordham University, wrote, "Common sense . . . tells us that the death penalty will deter murder, if anything can. People fear nothing more than death."

Dick Locher. Reprinted by permission: Tribune Media Services.

The author quotes religious authorities. Do you think these testimonials prove that these people approved of the death penalty? Why or why not?

Which propaganda technique is the author using in this paragraph?

Ernest van den Haag is a Distinguished Scholar at The Heritage Foundation and a law professor at Fordham University. He has also authored many books and articles on the death penalty. He is considered an authority on the death penalty. Does his testimonial support the author's argument that the death penalty is necessary?

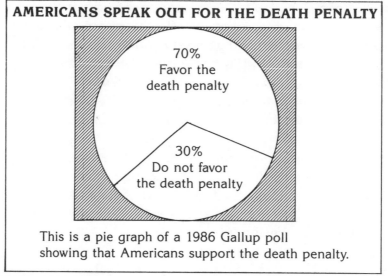

AMERICANS SPEAK OUT FOR THE DEATH PENALTY

70%
Favor the
death penalty

30%
Do not favor
the death penalty

This is a pie graph of a 1986 Gallup poll
showing that Americans support the death penalty.

SOURCE: 1986 Gallup poll

The author says the majority of Americans believe murderers deserve to die. He is implying that you should believe this too. Which propaganda technique is he using?

Does Senator McClellan's testimonial persuade you to agree with the author's argument that the death penalty is necessary? Why or why not?

Despite these arguments against the death penalty, the overwhelming majority of Americans believe murderers deserve to die for their crimes. Recent polls indicate that 72 percent of Americans are in favor of the death penalty. In fact, a majority of all groups, including blacks and whites, men and women, support the death penalty.

Some Americans have even said that there is no other just punishment for murder than the death penalty. In a debate on the subject, the late Democratic Senator John McClellan, referring to some particularly brutal murders, asked: "What other punishment is 'just' for a man . . . who would stab, strangle, and mutilate eight student nurses? What other punishment is 'just' for a band of social misfits who would invade the homes of people they had never even met and stab and hack to death a pregnant woman and her guests?"

It is time we reject the idea that murderers should not be executed. Most of these cruel killers cannot change their behavior. It is our duty to remove them from society so they can never kill again. And only the death penalty can ensure that they are removed.

Edward Koch, mayor of New York City, agrees. He said that we must apply the death penalty in certain cases if we are ever to have a civilized society where people do not kill each other.

Which propaganda technique is the author using here?

J. D. Crowe. Reprinted with permission.

Is the death penalty necessary?

The author first discusses his opponents' arguments against the death penalty and then tells why he thinks his opponents' arguments are weak. Find an example of this in the text.

What reasons does the author give for why we need to use the death penalty on murderers?

Identifying Propaganda Techniques

After reading the two viewpoints on whether the death penalty should be abolished, make a chart similar to the one made for Chip and Naomi on page 10. List one example of each propaganda technique for each author's viewpoint. A chart is started for you below:

Amnesty International:

TESTIMONIAL

A former warden of San Quentin Prison in California said that the death penalty is "a privilege of the poor."

Lincoln Review:

SCARE TACTIC

Murder has become an epidemic in our society.

After completing your chart, answer the following questions. Which article used the most propaganda techniques? Which article was the most convincing? Why? Which one did you personally agree with?

PREFACE: Should the Death Penalty Be Used for Some Crimes?

In the late 1800s, juries were required to impose the death penalty for various crimes including murders in which the killer meant to kill the victim. In the early 1900s, the laws changed. Jurors were allowed to consider the circumstances of the murder and then decide whether to sentence a murderer to death or to life in prison.

But many people wanted the death penalty ended altogether. They insisted that all executions were immoral and illegal. As a result, in 1967 the federal courts suspended all death sentences until the Supreme Court could decide whether the death penalty was legal.

In 1976, the Supreme Court decided that the death penalty was legal, but that it was at times handed out unfairly. This court established new rules and guidelines to be followed in murder cases to ensure that the death penalty is handed out fairly.

But many people feel that these new guidelines and regulations do not make the death penalty moral. They believe that killing another human being is always wrong. These people oppose the death penalty for all criminal cases.

On the other side are people who agree that some murderers do not deserve the death penalty. But these people disagree that the death penalty should never be used. They believe it is necessary to execute criminals who have committed particularly bad crimes. They argue that these criminals will not change their behavior and will always be a threat to society.

The next two viewpoints debate whether the death penalty should be required in some cases.

I am a convicted murderer. I am serving a sentence at the Kansas Correctional Institution. As a prisoner, I have lost many rights. But I still have the right to express my opinion. And I believe that the death penalty is the only appropriate punishment for certain crimes.

One of these crimes is murder committed for money. This includes murders committed during robberies and kidnappings. It also includes murders for hire.

Most murders are sad acts of anger. They involve people killing their friends and family during arguments. These murderers deserve to be treated with sympathy. But there are other killers who deserve no sympathy. These are the men and women who kill for money, without the slightest regard for human life. I know such people exist. I have lived among them.

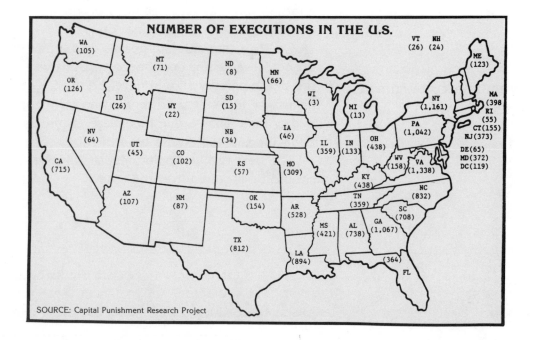

NUMBER OF EXECUTIONS IN THE U.S.

WA (105)
MT (71)
ND (8)
MN (66)
VT (26) NH (24)
ME (123)
OR (126)
ID (26)
WY (22)
SD (15)
WI (3)
MI (13)
NY (1,161)
MA (398)
RI (55)
PA (1,042)
CT (155)
NJ (373)
NV (64)
UT (45)
CO (102)
NB (34)
IA (46)
IL (359)
IN (133)
OH (438)
WV (158)
VA (1,338)
DE (65)
MD (372)
DC (119)
CA (715)
KS (57)
MO (309)
KY (438)
NC (832)
AZ (107)
NM (87)
OK (154)
AR (528)
TN (359)
SC (708)
MS (421)
AL (738)
GA (1,067)
TX (812)
LA (894)
FL (364)

SOURCE: Capital Punishment Research Project

I also support the death penalty for a prisoner who kills another person while in prison. These murderers are usually serving life sentences. They have nothing to lose by killing someone. Only the threat of the death penalty might stop them from killing fellow prisoners and guards.

Finally, I support the death penalty for murderers who commit more than one murder in a short period of time. For these people, murder has become a horrible hobby. I believe all these criminals deserve the death penalty for their crimes. Many other intelligent, thoughtful people agree with me. The Greek philosophers Plato and Aristotle supported the death penalty. So did St. Thomas Aquinas, Thomas More, the English statesman, and John Locke, the English philosopher.

The death penalty is fair punishment for some criminals. And it also saves the government money. It costs ten thousand dollars a year to keep a prisoner in jail until he dies. This amounts to five hundred thousand dollars or more for many prisoners. This is money taken from America's schools, hospitals, and the elderly.

A final reason for applying the death penalty is that it is actually more humane than keeping a person in prison for life. Sentencing a person to prison for life forces him or her to live without hope. He or she must endure unending years in an environment fit only for animals. A punishment that reduces a person to something less than human cannot be just.

I realize that most people do not like to think about the death penalty. It is unpleasant. But most modern societies do rob people of their lives. Our young die in far-off lands in wars. Their only "crime" is being too young to get out of going to war. We execute these young people by sending them to war. Why, then, don't we want to execute criminals?

Do you agree that people who commit more than one murder have chosen murder as a hobby? Is the author using a scare tactic?

The author is implying that intelligent, thoughtful people support the death penalty, and that you should too if you want to be considered intelligent and thoughtful. Which propaganda technique is the author using?

The author implies that if we keep prisoners in jail, we will not have enough money for our schools, hospitals, and elderly. Is he using a scare tactic? Why or why not?

Which crimes are punishable by death?

Name the three crimes Mr. Roome thinks deserve the death penalty. Do you agree? Do you think there are any crimes that deserve the death penalty? What are these crimes?

Editor's Note: This viewpoint is paraphrased from an article by Mary Meehan, a writer. In this viewpoint, Ms. Meehan discusses why she believes the death penalty should never be used. Some of the testimonials will be discussed in the focus box at the end of the reading.

Which propaganda technique is the author using in this paragraph?

Charles Peguy was a French poet and writer who wrote about people's rights. Does his testimonial persuade you to agree with the author that criminals should never be executed? Why or why not?

Criminals should never be given the death penalty for their crimes. There are many good reasons to oppose this form of punishment.

One of the most important reasons is that people have been executed for crimes they did not commit. Many of these people were found innocent after someone else admitted committing the crime.

Watt Espy, a researcher who has studied American executions, says he believes that ten innocent men were executed in Alabama alone. Mr. Espy cites names, dates, and other specifics of the cases. He adds that there are similar cases in almost every state.

What do we say after we have executed an innocent person? Do we write "I'm sorry" on his tombstone? What do we say to his widow and children?

The wrongful taking of a life by a country's government is a disgrace to the people of that country. We might consider Charles Peguy's words about the French case in which Captain Alfred Dreyfus was wrongly convicted of treason. Peguy said, "a single legal crime, a single dishonorable act will bring about the loss of one's honor, the dishonor of a whole people."

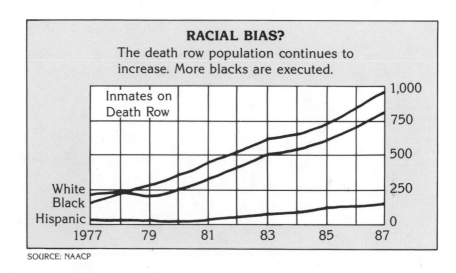

RACIAL BIAS?
The death row population continues to increase. More blacks are executed.

SOURCE: NAACP

Another reason for opposing the death penalty is that racial discrimination, or prejudice, is often used in deciding who dies and who does not. In the U.S., black people are given the death penalty more often than others. Of the 1,058 prisoners on death row in 1982, 42 percent were black. Only 12 percent of the U.S. population is black.

Walter Berns is a scholar who favors executing certain criminals. Yet he admits that judges and juries have used racial discrimination in handing out the death penalty. He told the Senate Judiciary Committee that the death penalty has been handed out to people in an unfair way in the United States.

Besides being unfair to blacks, the death penalty is also immoral. Many religions are against it. Former Iowa Senator Harold Hughes says the death penalty goes against the teaching of the Bible. He said, "'Thou shalt not kill' is the shortest of the Ten Commandments. . . . It is as clear . . . as the powerful thrust of chain lightning out of a dark summer sky." St. John, too, believed that no one has the right to kill another person. He wrote, "He that is without sin among you, let him cast the first stone."

The death penalty is immoral for another reason. It forces doctors to kill people. Doctors have to give the condemned prisoners shots of poison. This is wrong. Doctors are supposed to save people. The American Medical Association agrees. In 1980, the AMA said that doctors should not take part in an execution.

Many people oppose the death penalty. Even those people who are not "soft on crime" are against criminal execution. They do not think people have the right to play God. And they do not believe the government encourages respect for life when it kills people.

Albert Camus was a French writer and philosopher who died in 1960. He opposed the death penalty. Camus said, "We know enough to say that some crimes require severe punishment. We do not know enough to say when anyone should die." Camus was right.

Walter Berns is a scholar and writer who is considered an authority on the death penalty. Does his testimonial support the author's argument that the death penalty should never be applied?

Carol*Simpson/Rothco

The author says that many people oppose the death penalty. Is this a good reason for you to oppose it? Why or why not?

Is the death penalty wrong?

Ms. Meehan uses many testimonials in this viewpoint. Can you point out two of them in addition to the ones already mentioned? Analyze these two testimonials. Are either of them used deceptively? Why or why not?

Understanding Editorial Cartoons

Throughout this book you will see cartoons that illustrate the ideas in the viewpoints. Editorial cartoons are an effective and usually humorous way of presenting an opinion on an issue. Cartoonists, like writers, can use ways of persuading you that include propaganda techniques. While many cartoons are easy to understand, others, like the one below, require more thought.

Look at the two frames of the cartoon below. The cartoonist has drawn a frightening creature to represent people's urge to kill. What has been added to the second frame that does not appear in the first? Do you think the cartoonist approves or disapproves of the death penalty? Why? Does the cartoon persuade you to share the cartoonist's view on the death penalty? Why or why not?

'BAD'

© Miller/Rothco

'GOOD'

3

PREFACE: Does the Death Penalty Cause Murder?

A study was undertaken in the early 1980s to determine the effects of the death penalty on murder. The study found that between the years 1957 and 1965, when the death penalty was being used to punish murderers, 78,600 murders were committed in the U.S., and 337 people were executed. Between 1967 and 1976, when the Supreme Court suspended all executions, 159,600 murders were committed, and no people were executed.

People who favor the death penalty say that these statistics prove that the death penalty prevents murder. They point out that when people are executed for murder, the murder rate throughout the country decreases. On the other hand, when fewer people are executed for murder, the murder rate increases.

Other people argue that the death penalty increases murder. They acknowledge that when the number of executions goes up, the number of murders throughout the country goes down. But these people argue that important evidence is ignored. This evidence is that when an execution occurs in a certain city, the murder rate in that city goes up. This, they say, is proof that the death penalty encourages citizens to use violence as a solution to problems. The citizens believe that if the government can kill someone, it must be all right.

The next two viewpoints debate these issues. Pay close attention to the propaganda techniques the authors use.

Editor's Note: This viewpoint is paraphrased from an article by Louis Joylon West, chairman of the department of psychiatry and biobehavioral sciences at the University of California, Los Angeles Medical Center. In this viewpoint, Dr. West argues that the death penalty causes people to commit murder and that it should be ended.

Is the author using a propaganda technique in this paragraph? If so, which one?

The author says citizens accept killing as a solution to problems. Is he using a propaganda technique? If so, which one?

The death penalty should be abolished totally and permanently. There are many reasons why this is true. Perhaps the most difficult to understand is that the death penalty causes murder. The majority of scholars, governors, wardens, crime experts, jurists, and social scientists share this opinion.

When prisoners are executed, citizens accept killing as a solution to problems. This has been proved. Facts show that when an execution takes place, the murder rate goes up in that city. People think that if the government can kill someone, so can they.

But there is an even more specific way in which the death penalty causes murder. Some people who commit murder are actually trying to commit suicide. They believe if they kill someone they themselves will die because the government will execute them as punishment for their crime.

One example of this is a murderer named James French. French killed a driver who had stopped to pick him up while he was hitchhiking in Oklahoma. French asked to be executed for his crime. But he received a life sentence instead. French was outraged. After three years in prison, he strangled his cell mate. He admitted he did it just so he could be executed. In 1966, he got his wish. He was the only man executed during that year.

Sojourners/CPF. Reprinted with permission.

If the death penalty did not exist, the men French murdered would probably still be alive. It is likely that more people will be killed by murderers seeking their own deaths.

There are other examples of how the death penalty causes violence. One day a farmer walked into a roadside cafe in Texas. He aimed a shotgun at a man sitting at the lunch counter and killed him. He did not even know the man. When asked why he did it, he replied, "I was just tired of living."

In some cases, people who seek their own deaths even confess to a murder they did not commit. One such man was Joseph Shay. In 1966, Shay admitted that he had falsely confessed to an unsolved murder. He said he did it "because I wanted to die."

It is a fact that violent crime is part of our society. We are filled with sympathy for victims and their families. But the prisoner convicted of a violent crime is in prison. Society is safe from him. There is no reason to execute him.

There has been a trend toward ending the death penalty in countries in the Western world. These countries have fewer violent crimes than the United States. Most of these countries have many other laws that show mercy for their citizens.

Albert Camus, the French writer, opposed the death penalty. Camus believed the death penalty causes violence in societies. He said we have to end the death penalty if we ever hope to end war.

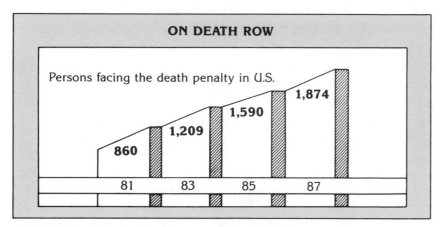

ON DEATH ROW

Persons facing the death penalty in U.S.

860 — 81
1,209 — 83
1,590 — 85
1,874 — 87

SOURCE: US Dept. of Justice. NAACP Legal Defense and Educational Fund

Is this a scare tactic? Why or why not?

Other countries are ending the death penalty. Is this a good enough reason for the United States to end it? Which propaganda technique is the author using?

Which propaganda technique is the author using in this paragraph?

Does the death penalty cause murder?

Mr. West cites two reasons for why the death penalty causes people to commit murder. What are these two reasons?

Editor's Note: This viewpoint is paraphrased from an article by Karl Spence. When he wrote this article, Mr. Spence was a student at Texas A & M University. Mr. Spence cites studies that prove that when the death penalty is enforced, murder decreases.

Does the author's evidence prove that slaughtering and robbing have become the American way of life? Is this a propaganda technique? If so, which one?

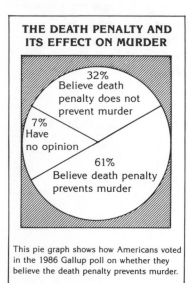

THE DEATH PENALTY AND ITS EFFECT ON MURDER

32% Believe death penalty does not prevent murder

7% Have no opinion

61% Believe death penalty prevents murder

This pie graph shows how Americans voted in the 1986 Gallup poll on whether they believe the death penalty prevents murder.

SOURCE: 1986 Gallup Poll

Is the author using a propaganda technique? If so, which one?

Violent crime has become a normal occurrence in the United States. Mass murder is so common that multiple killings often do not even make the headlines. The verb "to mug" has entered our vocabulary. Slaughtering and robbing American citizens has become part of the American way of life.

What is so horrifying is that people do not seem to care if their fellow citizens become crime victims. Skid row drunks are tortured to death. Young women are raped and strangled. Whole families are murdered in their beds, while the rest of us go on about our business.

In the fall of 1976, an elderly couple in New York City was robbed and tortured two different times in their own apartment. They finally hanged themselves. They said they did not want "to live in fear anymore."

There is still no agreement as to what causes crime in America. But there are many suggestions for how to prevent it.

One method of preventing crime is to defend ourselves from it. We can put multiple locks on our homes. We can use electronic security systems at airports and banks. We can try to control who owns guns. But these tactics make us feel like we are in constant danger. They make us think we have to be suspicious of our neighbors. Soon, we will believe we cannot trust anyone. This feeling that we cannot trust anyone is perhaps the most evil consequence of our failure to control crime.

The only thing that will prevent crime is punishment. For violent crimes, the death penalty is the answer.

Many American people oppose the death penalty. They hate the idea of execution as much as they hate crime. But the majority of Americans accept the death penalty as just punishment for some crimes. All Americans should support the death penalty.

People who oppose the death penalty say it does not prevent murder. But statistics prove that this is not true. A study of the relationship between the death penalty and murder shows that when more criminals are given the death penalty, fewer murders are committed. Likewise, when fewer criminals are executed, more murders are committed. For example, in 1957, there were 65 executions and 8,060 murders in the United States. In 1966, there was one execution and 10,920 murders, and in 1980, there were no executions and 23,040 murders.

Criminals do not want to die any more than anyone else. So, if they know they will receive the death penalty for killing someone, they probably will not do it.

A bloodbath is taking place in our country. In six months, more Americans are murdered than have died from the death penalty in this entire country. If we do not execute their murderers, these killings will continue. Until we begin to fight crime, every person who dies at a criminal's hands is the victim of our inaction. We must take responsibility for their deaths.

The late J. Edgar Hoover, former director of the F.B.I., agreed that we must take strong action against criminals. He said crime is a dangerous condition that will destroy our country if it is not ended soon.

Which propaganda technique is the author using in this paragraph?

Is the author using a propaganda technique in this paragraph? If so, which one?

Is this an example of a legitimate testimonial? Why or why not?

Are all testimonials the same?

Many of the testimonials you have read in these viewpoints are statements by people such as prison wardens and law professors who are somehow involved professionally with the criminal justice system. Other testimonials are by writers, poets, and philosophers who have no professional connection with the justice system, but who have spent much time thinking about and writing about solutions to social problems such as crime. Which group—the crime professionals or the writers and philosophers—do you think is in the best position to express informed opinions on the death penalty? Why?

Identifying Propaganda Techniques

This activity will allow you to practice identifying propaganda techniques. The statements below focus on the subject matter of this chapter—the effects of the death penalty on murder. Each statement is an example of bandwagon, scare tactic, or testimonial. Mark "B" next to any statement you believe is an example of bandwagon, "S" next to any statement you believe is a scare tactic, and "T" next to any statement you believe is a testimonial.

Answer

EXAMPLE: A warden at Garden State Prison said, "I have known people who have confessed to crimes they did not commit because they wanted to be executed."   T

1. Everyone in Mr. Lewis's first-grade class thinks the death penalty causes murder. You should agree with Mr. Lewis's class.   _____

2. Pope John Paul II had this to say about the death penalty, "It does not matter whether the fear of death would prevent murder, what matters is that killing people for any reason is immoral."   _____

3. If we let murderers back on the streets, chances are they will murder everyone in the U.S.   _____

4. J. Edgar Hoover, former director of the F.B.I., said that the death penalty prevents murder.   _____

5. Most intelligent people agree that killing a murderer is the only way to be sure he or she will not kill again. Anyone who disagrees with this is stupid.   _____

6. If we let the government keep killing people for crimes, someday it might start killing people for bad driving.   _____